Sirmione Travel Guide 2025

Things You Need To Know About Sirmione Before And After Traveling. The Ultimate Guide to Touring Sirmione, adventure.

Billy L ALLEN

Table Of Contents

Chapter 1. Introduction
Welcome to Sirmione

Chapter 2. Getting to Know Sirmione
Overview of Sirmione
History of Sirmione
Geography and Climate

Chapter 3. Sirmione's Historical Treasures
Scaliger Castle: Sentinel of the Peninsula
Grotte di Catullo: Roman Ruins by the Lake
Church of San Pietro in Mavino

Chapter 4. Natural Beauty and Outdoor Activities
Lake Garda: Jewel of Northern Italy
Thermal Spas: Healing Waters of Sirmione
Monte Baldo: Adventure in the Alps
Lakeside Promenades and Gardens

Chapter 5. Cultural Attractions and Events
Festivals and Events Calendar
Art Galleries and Museums
Cultural Heritage Sites

Chapter 6. Culinary Delights of Sirmione
Traditional Cuisine of Lake Garda

Olive Oil and Wine Tasting
Best Restaurants and Local Eateries

Chapter 7. Practical Information for Visitors
Transportation in Sirmione
Accommodation Options
Shopping and Souvenirs
Safety Tips and Emergency Contacts

Chapter 8. Itineraries and Day Trips
One-Day Itinerary: Highlights of Sirmione
Two-Day Adventure: Exploring Lake Garda
Beyond Sirmione: Day Trips to Nearby Attractions

Chapter 9. Tips for a Memorable Stay
Photography Tips for Capturing Sirmione's Beauty
Packing Essentials for Different Seasons

Chapter 10. Conclusion
Farewell to Sirmione

Appendix
Glossary of Italian Terms
Map

Chapter 1. Introduction

Welcome to Sirmione

Welcome to Sirmione, a beautiful location set on the southern banks of Lake Garda, Italy's biggest lake. This lovely town, steeped in history and surrounded by spectacular natural beauty, welcomes guests with open arms, encouraging them to immerse themselves in its rich tapestry of culture, gastronomy, and outdoor experiences.

As you arrive at Sirmione, you'll be met by the towering silhouette of Scaliger Castle, a medieval castle that remains a witness to the town's illustrious history. Built-in the 13th century by the strong Scaliger family, the castle's crenellated walls and towers generate a feeling of awe and mystery, hinting at the centuries of history that lay behind its stone walls.

But Sirmione is more than simply a historic site; it's a living village with a dynamic cultural scene that resonates with people from across the globe. From art galleries highlighting local talent to busy markets packed with exquisite items, there's always something new and fascinating to discover around every turn.

One of the delights of visiting Sirmione is the chance to explore its natural treasures, from the crystal-clear waters of Lake Garda to the green hillsides that surround the town. Whether you're enjoying a leisurely walk along the lakeside promenade or starting on a picturesque trip through the Monte Baldo nature reserve, you'll be fascinated by the sheer beauty of your surroundings.

Of course, no visit to Sirmione would be complete without partaking in its gastronomic pleasures. From classic trattorias offering substantial pasta meals to waterfront eateries specializing in fresh seafood, the town's eclectic culinary culture provides something to tickle every pallet. Be sure to taste the local delights, such as olive oil from the adjacent orchards and wine from the vineyards that dot the area.

As you commence your tour through Sirmione, take a minute to absorb the slower pace of life and relish the simple pleasures that exist in this exquisite area. Whether you're drinking a cappuccino at a sidewalk café, savoring the sunset over the lake, or just meandering the cobblestone streets in search of hidden treasures, you'll discover that Sirmione has a way of grabbing your heart and leaving you craving for more.

So welcome to Sirmione, where history, natural beauty, and cultural appeal mix to offer an amazing experience. Whether you're here for a day, a week, or a lifetime, you'll quickly find why this fascinating town has caught the imagination of tourists for generations.

Chapter 2. Getting to Know Sirmione

Overview of Sirmione

Getting to know Sirmione is like unraveling the threads of a magnificent tapestry, each strand woven with history, natural beauty, and cultural importance. Situated on a tiny peninsula protruding into Lake Garda, Sirmione is a charming village that epitomizes the spirit of Italian charm.

At the heart of Sirmione lies its ancient town, a maze of small cobblestone lanes dotted with colorful houses covered with flower boxes. As you travel through the labyrinth of alleys, you'll see centuries-old churches, lovely piazzas, and secret courtyards waiting to be found. Each corner offers a fresh layer of the town's history, from the Roman remains of the Grotte di Catullo to the medieval fortification of Scaliger Castle, which stands guard at the entrance to the peninsula.

Surrounded by the turquoise waters of Lake Garda, Sirmione has some of the most stunning vistas in Italy. The dazzling expanse of the lake spreads as far as the eye can reach, framed by the craggy peaks of the Alps in the background. From the lakeside promenade, you may watch as sailboats skim over the water, their white sails blowing in the air, or just absorb in the calm of the setting as the sun sets below the horizon, creating a golden light over the water.

But Sirmione is more than just a gorgeous postcard; it's a live, breathing village with a bustling cultural scene. Throughout the year, the town comes alive with festivals and events celebrating everything from music and art to cuisine and wine. Whether you're eating local specialties at a culinary festival or attending a classical performance in the courtyard of Scaliger Castle, you'll discover that there's always something going on in Sirmione to delight and inspire.

Of course, no visit to Sirmione would be complete without partaking in its gastronomic pleasures. From classic trattorias offering handmade pasta meals to trendy waterfront eateries specializing in fresh seafood, the town's eating scene delivers a feast for the senses. Be sure to taste the local delicacies, such as risotto di pesce (seafood risotto) or torta di Limone (lemon cake), and wash it down with a drink of locally made wine or olive oil.

As you explore Sirmione, you'll quickly learn that the town has a way of stealing your heart and leaving you craving for more. Whether you're walking the old alleyways of the historic center, relaxing on the beaches of Lake Garda, or just sipping a gelato in the afternoon sun, you'll find that Sirmione is a location where every moment is a treasure waiting to be found.

History of Sirmione

To properly comprehend the essence of Sirmione, one must dig into its rich and storied past, a trip that spans millennia and involves the rise and fall of empires, the ebb and flow of trade and commerce, and the undying spirit of its people.

The history of Sirmione extends back to prehistoric times, with signs of human occupancy going as far back as the Neolithic era. However, it was during the Roman period that Sirmione started to prosper, due to its strategic position on the beaches of Lake Garda. The Romans saw the town's potential as a strategic outpost and erected a series of fortifications to protect it from invaders, including the magnificent villa known as the Grotte di Catullo, which still exists as a witness to the town's historic history.

In the centuries that followed, Sirmione continued to grow as a hub of trade and business, due to its proximity to the busy port towns of northern Italy. Merchants from around the Mediterranean would travel to Sirmione to trade items such as olive oil, wine, and pottery, enriching the town's cultural tapestry with influences from far-flung regions.

However, Sirmione's fortunes took a turn for the worse throughout the Middle Ages, when the area was thrown into a series of battles and power struggles between competing city-states. The town was besieged and ravaged many times by raiding armies, leaving its once-prosperous streets in ruins.

Despite these trials, Sirmione managed to persevere, due in part to the perseverance of its population and the sponsorship of great aristocratic families like the Scaligeri. Under the tenure of the Scaligeri family, Sirmione saw a period of rebirth and prosperity, with the building of the renowned Scaliger Castle and other architectural wonders that still exist today as emblems of the town's medieval legacy.

In the decades that followed, Sirmione continued to grow, embracing new technology and cultural influences while keeping its ageless beauty and character. Today, the town remains a living witness to its rich and diversified past, with ancient ruins set against contemporary conveniences and a thriving cultural scene that resonates with people from across the globe.

As you tour Sirmione and immerse yourself in its fabled past, you'll realize that the echoes of history are everywhere, from the ancient Roman remains to the medieval strongholds and Renaissance palaces that dot the landscape. Each stone tells a tale, and each street has a mystery, urging you to solve the secrets of this wonderful town and find the real essence of Sirmione.

Geography and Climate

Understanding the topography and climate of Sirmione is necessary to understand the appeal and beauty of this charming town located on the beaches of Lake Garda. Situated in the Lombardy area of northern Italy, Sirmione possesses a small peninsula that extends into the southernmost portion of the lake, producing a unique and attractive environment that has attracted travelers for ages.

The topography of Sirmione is characterized by its spectacular natural surroundings, with Lake Garda acting as the main point of the town's scenery. As the biggest lake in Italy, Lake Garda features crystal-clear waters that glitter in the sunshine, framed by the beautiful peaks of the Alps in the background. The lake offers a beautiful background to Sirmione, allowing inhabitants and tourists alike a quiet getaway from the rush and bustle of contemporary life.

In addition to its gorgeous lakeside backdrop, Sirmione is also endowed with a broad assortment of natural characteristics, including lush foliage, rolling slopes, and attractive vineyards. The town's Mediterranean environment further accentuates its natural beauty, with moderate winters, sunny summers, and an abundance of sunlight throughout the year.

During the summer months, Sirmione comes alive with bustle as visitors throng to the town to soak up the sun, swim in the lake, and explore its various attractions. Temperatures normally vary from the mid-70s to the mid-80s Fahrenheit (about 24-30 degrees Celsius), making it the best season to enjoy outdoor activities such as hiking, cycling, and boating.

of contrast, the winter months of Sirmione are quite moderate, with temperatures averaging in the 40s to 50s Fahrenheit (about 5-10 degrees Celsius). While the town may encounter periodic showers and freezing winds during this season, it remains a popular location for those seeking a calm getaway away from the masses.

No matter the season, Sirmione's topography and climate offer the ideal background for a broad choice of outdoor excursions and cultural encounters. Whether you're visiting the historic remains of Scaliger Castle, resting in the thermal baths, or just walking along the lakeside promenade, you'll discover that Sirmione's natural beauty and Mediterranean temperature offer an enchanting environment that is guaranteed to make a lasting impression.

Chapter 3. Sirmione's Historical Treasures

Scaliger Castle: Sentinel of the Peninsula

Scaliger Castle sits as a fearsome guard at the entrance to Sirmione's short peninsula, demanding attention with its high walls, robust towers, and commanding location overlooking Lake Garda. This towering stronghold, also known as the Castello Scaligero, is one of the most prominent monuments in Sirmione and serves as a symbol of the town's rich history and medieval past.

Constructed in the 13th century by the powerful Scaligeri dynasty, who controlled most of northern Italy throughout the Middle Ages, Scaliger Castle was constructed both as a defensive fortress and a symbol of the family's riches and power. Its strategic position at the tip of the peninsula provided it a great vantage point for monitoring and regulating entry to the town, as well as fighting against prospective attackers.

The castle's construction is a monument to the military might of the Scaligeri, with its massive stone walls, battlements, and towers meant to survive even the most desperate siege. The main entrance to the castle is accessible by a drawbridge across a moat, contributing to its fearsome look and conjuring images of knights and medieval battles.

Inside the castle walls, visitors may explore a maze of apartments, chambers, and corridors that provide insights into the everyday lives of its occupants throughout the Middle Ages. Highlights include the magnificent main courtyard, the dark dungeons where captives were formerly kept captive, and the tower rooms that give panoramic views of the surrounding terrain.

One of the most outstanding characteristics of Scaliger Castle is its five towers, each of which has its distinct design and function. The largest tower, known as the Mastio or keep, served as the dwelling of the castle's ruler and gave spectacular views of the lake and surrounding landscape. The other towers housed troops, stored supplies, and acted as observation positions, offering important protection in times of battle.

Throughout its long history, Scaliger Castle has played a major role in defining the fate of Sirmione, seeing triumphs and tragedies, wars and peace, and the ebb and flow of life on the shores of Lake Garda. Today, it remains a testimony to the continuing history of the Scaligeri family and a symbol of Sirmione's medieval past, encouraging tourists to go back in time and experience the beauty of this historic castle firsthand.

Grotte di Catullo: Roman Ruins by the Lake

The Grotte di Catullo, located on the magnificent shores of Lake Garda, remains as quiet witness to the grandeur of ancient Rome and the lasting memory of one of its most brilliant writers. These spectacular Roman remains, situated on the northern extremity of Sirmione's peninsula, are a monument to the town's rich history and cultural legacy, affording tourists a fascinating peek into the past.

Believed to be the remnants of a great Roman villa dating back to the 1st century BC, the Grotte di Catullo is one of the biggest and most significant archeological sites in northern Italy. Named for the Roman poet Gaius Valerius Catullus, who is claimed to have possessed a villa in the vicinity, the location is steeped in myth, folklore, and historical intrigue.

As you approach the Grotte di Catullo, you'll be impressed by the sheer magnitude and majesty of the ruins, which spread over a huge plateau overlooking the blue waters of Lake Garda. The ruins of the villa's foundations, columns, and walls are strewn throughout the terrain, presenting tantalizing hints of its previous majesty and splendor.

One of the most outstanding characteristics of the Grotte di Catullo is the panoramic vista it affords over Lake Garda and the surrounding area. From the lofty vantage point of the ruins, visitors may observe the glittering waters of the lake, framed by the rocky peaks of the Alps in the distance, offering a stunning setting for exploration and contemplation.

As you explore amid the ruins, you'll uncover signs of the villa's past grandeur, from the delicate mosaic flooring to the elaborate marble columns and sculptures that once decorated its hallways. Archaeological digs have discovered evidence of sumptuous living chambers, magnificent gardens, and complex plumbing systems, revealing insights into the everyday lives of the villa's residents at the height of the Roman Empire.

Despite the passage of time and the ravages of nature, the Grotte di Catullo remains an intriguing site for history aficionados, art lovers, and inquisitive tourists alike. Its ageless beauty and historical importance make it a must-visit destination in Sirmione, affording a window into the past and a glimpse of the lasting heritage of ancient Rome. Whether you're exploring the ruins, appreciating the panoramic vistas, or just soaking in the ambiance, the Grotte di Catullo is guaranteed to create a lasting impact and inspire your imagination.

Church of San Pietro in Mavino

The Church of San Pietro in Mavino, located within the scenic environment of Sirmione, serves as a witness to the town's rich religious legacy and architectural magnificence. This old cathedral, steeped in history and tradition, is a treasure mine of artistic and cultural value, beckoning visitors to go on a trip through time and learn the mysteries of its legendary past.

Believed to have been established in the 8th century, the Church of San Pietro in Mavino is one of the oldest churches in Sirmione and a unique example of Lombard Romanesque architecture in the area. Its basic but magnificent façade, distinguished by a succession of rounded arches and geometric motifs, represents the architectural style of the period and looks at the religious activities and beliefs of medieval Italy.

As you go inside the church, you'll be met with a feeling of peace and respect, as shafts of sunshine flood through stained glass windows, bathing the interior with a warm and ethereal glow. The nave is embellished with murals, paintings, and sculptures that show episodes from the life of Saint Peter, the patron saint of the church, as well as other biblical characters and saints loved by the devout.

One of the most prominent characteristics of the Church of San Pietro in Mavino is its old bell tower, which rises magnificently above the surrounding terrain, affording panoramic views of Sirmione and the sparkling waters of Lake Garda. Dating back to the 12th century, the bell tower is a masterpiece of medieval architecture and workmanship, with its solid stone walls and elaborate carvings standing as a tribute to the skill and inventiveness of its architects.

Throughout its long history, the Church of San Pietro in Mavino has been a destination of worship, pilgrimage, and thought for the faithful of Sirmione and beyond. Its walls have watched weddings, baptisms, and burials, as well as moments of joy, sadness, and spiritual enlightenment. Today, the church continues to serve as a beacon of faith and a symbol of the continuous relationship between past and present, allowing people to stop, think, and connect with the holy.

Whether you're attracted to its historic architecture, its rich artistic legacy, or its spiritual importance, the Church of San Pietro in Mavino provides a unique and remarkable experience that is guaranteed to make a lasting impact on all who come. So come, go inside, and explore the timeless beauty and spiritual secrets of this ancient gem situated in the heart of Sirmione.

Chapter 4. Natural Beauty and Outdoor Activities

Lake Garda: Jewel of Northern Italy

Lake Garda, frequently touted as the gem of northern Italy, captivates tourists with its spectacular natural beauty, various landscapes, and richness of outdoor activities. Nestled between the beautiful peaks of the Alps to the north and the rolling hills of the Lombardy and Veneto regions to the south, Lake Garda is the biggest lake in Italy and a paradise for nature lovers, outdoor enthusiasts, and adventure seekers alike.

Stretching over 50 kilometers in length and encompassing three provinces – Brescia, Verona, and Trentino – Lake Garda has a vast assortment of sceneries, from craggy cliffs and rocky shorelines to sandy beaches and lush olive orchards. Its crystal-clear waters glisten in the sunshine, reflecting the ever-changing colors of the sky and neighboring mountains, offering a stunning setting for exploration and relaxation.

One of the delights of visiting Lake Garda is the ability to explore its scenic coastline, which is lined with attractive lakeside towns and villages, each with its special charm and character. From the historic alleyways of Sirmione to the colorful ports of Malcesine and Riva del Garda, there's always something new and thrilling to discover around every turn.

But Lake Garda is more than simply a picturesque background; it's also a paradise for outdoor activities and adventure sports. Whether you're an enthusiastic hiker, biker, water sports enthusiast, or just like soaking up the sun on a sandy beach, Lake Garda provides something for everyone.

For hiking aficionados, the Monte Baldo mountain range, which rises sharply from the eastern coast of Lake Garda, provides a network of magnificent paths that snake through woods, meadows, and alpine pastures, affording panoramic views of the lake and surrounding countryside.

Water sports aficionados will find plenty of options for adventure on Lake Garda, with activities including sailing, windsurfing, kiteboarding, and kayaking accessible year-round. The lake's consistent breezes and beautiful waters make it a great location for sailing enthusiasts, while its protected bays and coves give the perfect backdrop for swimming and snorkeling.

Those wanting a more leisurely pace may just relax on one of the lake's numerous beaches, where they can soak up the sun, swim in the cool waters, or have a picnic with family and friends. For those wishing to immerse themselves in the region's cultural and gastronomic legacy, there are countless towns and villages along the lake's banks where visitors may taste local specialties, tour historic sites, and enjoy the warm hospitality of the inhabitants.

Whether you're seeking adventure, leisure, or cultural immersion, Lake Garda provides an extraordinary experience that is guaranteed to make a lasting impact on all who come. So come, see the treasure of northern Italy, and enjoy the timeless beauty and endless mysteries of Lake Garda.

Thermal Spas: Healing Waters of Sirmione

Nestled along the shores of Lake Garda, the thermal baths of Sirmione lure guests with their promise of relaxation, renewal, and healing. These natural hot springs, famed for their therapeutic benefits, have been drawing people for generations, lured by the soothing warmth of the waters and the calm beauty of their surroundings.

The thermal spas of Sirmione owe their existence to the region's unique geological characteristics, which have generated a network of subterranean hot springs that bubble to the surface, carrying with them a plethora of minerals and trace elements that are said to have therapeutic effects. These mineral-rich waters are supposed to help treat a range of diseases, including rheumatism, arthritis, and skin disorders, making it a popular destination for individuals seeking relief from pain and suffering.

As you immerse yourself in the warm waters of the thermal baths, you'll feel the worries and strains of everyday life melt away, replaced with a sensation of profound relaxation and well-being. The mild heat of the water calms sore muscles and joints, while the mineral-rich composition nourishes the skin, leaving it soft, smooth, and luminous.

But the advantages of the thermal baths extend beyond simply physical healing; they also provide a sanctuary for the mind and soul, giving a calm getaway from the rush and bustle of contemporary life. Surrounded by lush gardens, picturesque vistas, and quiet surroundings, the thermal baths of Sirmione provide a tranquil refuge where guests may escape the demands of the outside world and reconnect with themselves and nature.

In addition to its medicinal characteristics, the thermal springs of Sirmione also provide a multitude of leisure activities for guests to enjoy. Whether you're resting in a thermal pool, indulging in a spa treatment, or just basking in the sun on a lakeside balcony, there's something for everyone to enjoy.

For those seeking adventure, the surrounding region provides lots of chances for outdoor sports, from hiking and cycling to sailing and windsurfing. For those interested in exploring the region's rich cultural legacy, there are countless historic sites, museums, and galleries to visit, offering a fascinating peek into the history and culture of Sirmione and the surrounding area.

Whether you're seeking health, relaxation, or adventure, the thermal baths of Sirmione provide a unique and fascinating experience that is guaranteed to make a lasting impact on everyone who comes. So come, immerse yourself in the therapeutic waters, and explore the natural beauty and outdoor activities that await in this wonderful corner of Italy.

Monte Baldo: Adventure in the Alps

Nestled on the eastern bank of Lake Garda, Monte Baldo rises magnificently from the water's edge, allowing explorers and nature lovers alike an unequaled chance to immerse themselves in the stunning splendor of the Alps. This enormous mountain range, frequently referred to as the "Garden of Europe," features a vast variety of landscapes, from lush forests and alpine meadows to craggy peaks and precipitous cliffs, offering a playground for outdoor lovers and a haven for animals.

At the heart of Monte Baldo sits the Monte Baldo Regional Park, a huge protected area encompassing over 200 square kilometers of pure nature. Here, tourists may explore a network of picturesque paths that snake through woods of beech, chestnut, and pine, affording spectacular views of Lake Garda and the surrounding countryside. Along the journey, hikers may witness a variety of species, including deer, chamois, and even the rare golden eagle swooping above.

One of the attractions of visiting Monte Baldo is the ability to trek to its highest peak, which gives panoramic views of the whole area. Visitors may reach the peak by using the Monte Baldo Cable Car, which whisks visitors from the lakeside village of Malcesine to the top of the mountain in only a few minutes. From there, guests may go on a leisurely walk around the top routes, taking in the sweeping panoramas of Lake Garda, the Dolomites, and the Adamello-Presanella mountain range in the distance.

For those wanting a more adventurous experience, Monte Baldo provides a choice of outdoor activities to suit every taste and ability level. Mountain cyclists will discover a network of exciting paths that meander through the mountain's challenging topography, while rock climbers may try their abilities on the steep limestone cliffs that dot the area. In the winter months, the mountain changes into a snowy paradise, providing options for skiing, snowboarding, and snowshoeing.

But arguably the greatest draw of Monte Baldo resides in its natural beauty, which has inspired painters, authors, and poets for generations. From the delicate wildflowers that blanket the meadows in spring to the flaming colors of the fall leaves, the mountain's ever-changing sceneries are a feast for the senses and a source of infinite inspiration.

Whether you're seeking adventure, leisure, or just a chance to reconnect with nature, Monte Baldo delivers a unique experience that is guaranteed to have a lasting effect on all who come. So come, see the beauties of the Alps, and discover the natural beauty and outdoor activities that await Monte Baldo.

Lakeside Promenades and Gardens

As the soft wind transports the aroma of
blossoming flowers and the sound of lapping waves,
visitors to Lake Garda find themselves attracted to
the stunning lakeside promenades and gardens
along the beaches, creating a calm refuge of natural
beauty and solitude.

Strolling down the promenades, flanked by
towering cypress trees and vivid bougainvillea, one
can't help but be captured by the stunning vistas of
the turquoise waters of Lake Garda reaching out to
the horizon. The sun-kissed waters glisten in the
sunshine, producing a brilliant reflection that
dances over the surface, while sailboats glide
effortlessly across the lake, their billowing sails
giving a sense of elegance to the picture.

As you meander down the promenades, you'll meet
a kaleidoscope of hues and smells, as lush gardens
explode with vivid blossoms and aromatic herbs.
From the delicate petals of roses and lilies to the
fragrant perfume of lavender and rosemary, the air
is alive with the spirit of spring, asking you to stop,
breathe deeply, and relish the moment.

Along the trip, you may stumble across lonely alcoves and secret walkways, where benches beg tired visitors to stop and think among the grandeur of nature. Here, you may remain awhile, listening to the subtle rustling of leaves in the air and the distant hum of bees among the flowers, letting a sensation of calm and tranquility wash over you.

But the lakeside promenades and gardens provide more than just a feast for the senses; they also provide a background for a range of outdoor sports and leisure pastimes. Whether you're taking a leisurely bike ride along the lakefront, practicing yoga on the grassy meadows, or just having a picnic with family and friends, there's something for everyone to enjoy among the natural beauty of Lake Garda.

In the evening, as the sun sets below the horizon and the sky is painted in colors of pink and gold, the lakeside promenades and gardens take on a lovely aura, as glittering lights illuminate the paths and the sound of laughing and music fills the air. It's a time for romance and enchantment, as lovers wander hand in hand under the starlit sky, enthralled in the beauty of the moment.

Whether you're seeking peace and introspection or adventure and excitement, the lakeside promenades and gardens of Lake Garda provide a refuge for the spirit and a haven for the senses, beckoning you to leave the hustle and bustle of daily life and reconnect with the beauty of the natural world. So come, take a walk along the beaches of Lake Garda, and experience the enchantment that lies among the lakeside promenades and gardens.

Chapter 5. Cultural Attractions and Events

Festivals and Events Calendar

The festivals and events calendar of Sirmione is a vivid tapestry woven with the threads of history, culture, and celebration, allowing visitors a unique chance to immerse themselves in the rich legacy and dynamic spirit of this delightful town. Throughout the year, Sirmione plays home to a broad assortment of festivals, events, and cultural attractions that exhibit the finest of local art, music, food, and customs, inviting tourists from near and far to participate in the celebrations and make memorable memories.

One of the highlights of Sirmione's events calendar is the annual Festival dei Fiori, or Flower Festival, which takes place in the springtime when the town's gardens burst into bloom with vivid hues and fragrant petals. During the festival, the streets of Sirmione are converted into a floral paradise, as residents and tourists alike congregate to enjoy spectacular floral displays, engage in flower arrangement workshops, and take part in parades and processions commemorating the beauty of nature.

In the summer months, Sirmione comes alive with a frenzy of song, dancing, and celebration, as the town plays home to a variety of music festivals, concerts, and outdoor performances. From classical concerts in the courtyard of Scaliger Castle to jazz festivals on the beaches of Lake Garda, there's something for every musical taste and preference, with performances by local and worldwide performers alike.

For food connoisseurs, the Sagra del Pesce, or Fish Festival, is a must-visit event, held yearly in the summer months to celebrate the wealth of the lake and the culinary traditions of the area. During the festival, local fisherman demonstrate their catch of the day, which is then cooked and served up in a range of tasty meals, from classic seafood pasta to grilled fish on a skewer. Visitors may also enjoy live music, dancing, and other entertainment while they eat al fresco on the banks of Lake Garda.

As fall arrives upon Sirmione, the town's streets come alive with the sights, sounds, and fragrances of the annual Olive Oil Festival, which celebrates the olive harvest and the long legacy of olive oil manufacturing in the area. During the festival, visitors may taste a range of olive oils from local producers, learn about the olive oil manufacturing process, and participate in olive oil tastings and cookery demonstrations.

Throughout the year, Sirmione also plays home to a range of cultural events, including art exhibits, theater performances, and literary readings, which highlight the skills of local artists and authors and give a platform for creative expression and inquiry. Whether you're a fan of music, cuisine, art, or literature, there's something for everyone to enjoy on Sirmione's festivals and events calendar, affording a unique chance to explore the rich cultural legacy and dynamic spirit of this charming town.

Art Galleries and Museums

Sirmione's art galleries and museums serve as cultural lighthouses, showcasing the town's rich history, artistic legacy, and creative energy. From ancient relics to modern masterpieces, these institutions provide visitors an insight into the history, present, and future of Sirmione's thriving arts scene, affording a unique chance to experience the town's cultural identity and creative heritage.

One of the town's most distinctive cultural attractions is the Museo Archeologico di Sirmione, or the Archaeological Museum of Sirmione, which is situated behind the magnificent walls of Scaliger Castle. Here, visitors may go on a journey through time, studying the ancient history of Sirmione and the surrounding area via a wide collection of relics, artworks, and archaeological findings. Highlights of the museum's collection include Roman sculptures, ceramics, and mosaics, as well as objects from the prehistoric and medieval eras, affording a fascinating view into the town's illustrious history.

For art connoisseurs, the Galleria d'Arte Moderna e Contemporanea, or Gallery of Modern and Contemporary Art, presents a selected collection of works by local and international artists, encompassing several genres and materials. From paintings and sculptures to multimedia installations and conceptual art, the gallery displays the richness and originality of Sirmione's creative community, giving a platform for young and experienced artists alike to share their ideas with the world.

In addition to its museums and galleries, Sirmione is also home to a variety of cultural institutions and historic buildings that showcase the town's creative past and cultural traditions. The Chiesa di San Pietro in Mavino, for example, is not only a place of worship but also holds a collection of medieval paintings and religious items that give insights into the town's religious and cultural past.

Throughout the year, Sirmione plays home to a range of cultural events and exhibits that highlight the skills of local artists and musicians and give opportunities for visitors to connect with the arts. From art fairs and music festivals to theater performances and literary readings, there's always something going on in Sirmione to inspire, amuse, and inform.

Whether you're a fan of art, history, or culture, Sirmione's art galleries and museums provide a multitude of possibilities to discover the town's rich cultural past and creative legacy. So come, walk inside, and explore the beauty, creativity, and passion that constitute Sirmione's dynamic arts scene.

Cultural Heritage Sites

Sirmione's cultural heritage sites serve as living testaments to the town's rich history, architectural grandeur, and cultural relevance, allowing visitors a look into the past and a fuller understanding of the forces that have created the town's character over the years. From ancient ruins to medieval fortifications, these places are a treasure trove of historical and cultural riches, encouraging tourists to go on a trip through time and learn the mysteries of Sirmione's fascinating history.

One of the most recognizable cultural heritage monuments in Sirmione is Scaliger Castle, a beautiful fortification that stands guard at the entrance to the town's short peninsula. Built-in the 13th century by the strong Scaligeri family, the castle is a marvel of medieval architecture, with its high stone walls, robust towers, and towering battlements conjuring visions of knights and gallant warriors. Inside the castle walls, visitors may explore a maze of rooms, courtyards, and corridors, including the eerie dungeons where captives were formerly kept, affording insights into the castle's military and political past.

Another must-visit cultural heritage site in Sirmione is the Grotte di Catullo, or the Catullus Caves, a large ancient complex situated on the northern extremity of the peninsula. Believed to be the remnants of a splendid Roman villa dating back to the 1st century BC, the Grotte di Catullo is one of the biggest and most significant Roman monuments in northern Italy, with its ruins affording a fascinating view into the everyday life and culture of ancient Rome. Visitors may examine the remnants of the villa's foundations, columns, and walls, as well as enjoy panoramic views of Lake Garda and the surrounding countryside from the lofty vantage point of the ruins.

In addition to these renowned structures, Sirmione is also home to a variety of additional cultural heritage sites and historic landmarks that highlight the town's rich architectural legacy and cultural traditions. The Chiesa di San Pietro in Mavino, for example, is one of the oldest churches in Sirmione, dating back to the 8th century, and has a collection of medieval paintings and religious relics that give insights into the town's religious and cultural past. Similarly, the house Romana, a Roman house situated on the banks of Lake Garda, provides tourists a peek into the sumptuous lifestyle of ancient Roman nobility, with its well-preserved mosaics, frescoes, and hot baths.

Throughout the year, Sirmione's cultural heritage sites play home to a range of events, exhibits, and cultural activities that reflect the town's rich history and cultural traditions. From guided tours and historical reenactments to art exhibits and music performances, there's always something going on in Sirmione to inspire, educate, and delight visitors of all ages.

Whether you're a history buff, an architecture enthusiast, or simply curious about the past, Sirmione's cultural heritage sites offer a wealth of opportunities to explore the town's rich history and cultural heritage, providing a deeper understanding of the forces that have shaped the town's identity and character over the centuries. So come, travel back in time, and enjoy the beauty, mystery, and enchantment of Sirmione's cultural heritage sites.

Chapter 6. Culinary Delights of Sirmione

Traditional Cuisine of Lake Garda

The traditional food of Lake Garda is a gourmet adventure that embodies the rich culinary history and cultural variety of the area, delivering a tempting array of tastes, textures, and smells that excite the senses and satisfy the palette. From fresh seafood and locally produced fruit to substantial pasta meals and indulgent sweets, the cuisine of Lake Garda embraces the abundance of the land and the sea, while paying attention to the traditions and rituals that have created the region's culinary character over the years.

One of the distinguishing elements of Lake Garda's cuisine is its focus on fresh, seasonal ingredients derived from local growers and craftsmen. Fishermen sail the waters of the lake in quest of the day's catch, which includes a variety of freshwater species such as perch, trout, and whitefish, as well as the coveted lake sardines known as "luscious" and "coregone." These fish are commonly grilled, roasted, or fried and served with a squeeze of lemon and a drizzle of local olive oil, enabling their natural tastes to show through.

In addition to fish, Lake Garda's food also offers an abundance of locally produced fruits and vegetables, including tomatoes, zucchini, eggplant, and peppers, which are utilized to make a range of excellent meals such as risotto, pasta, and salads. Olive oil, another mainstay of the area, is used widely in cooking, providing richness and depth of flavor to many traditional meals.

One of the most emblematic meals of Lake Garda is "risotto al pesce," a creamy risotto cooked with fish broth, white wine, and a variety of shellfish such as shrimp, clams, and mussels. This substantial meal is a favorite among residents and tourists alike, with its rich, savory tastes and creamy texture that is both soothing and gratifying.

Another famous dish is "trota alla gardesana," or Lake Garda-style trout, which is marinated in a combination of olive oil, garlic, lemon, and herbs before being grilled or baked to perfection. The result is a delicate, delicious fish that works wonderfully with a bottle of local wine and a side of fresh veggies.

Of course, no supper at Lake Garda would be complete without dessert, and the area provides a range of sweet delicacies to please even the most discerning sweet taste. One of the most popular sweets is "torta di mele," or apple cake, prepared with locally produced apples and sweetened with cinnamon, nutmeg, and vanilla. This rich, savory cake is the ideal finish to a good dinner, particularly when served warm with a dollop of freshly whipped cream.

Throughout the year, Sirmione's restaurants, trattorias, and osterias highlight the finest of Lake Garda's traditional food, allowing tourists an opportunity to sample the flavors of the area and feel the warmth and friendliness of its people. Whether you're eating on a patio overlooking the lake or enjoying street food from a local market, the traditional cuisine of Lake Garda is guaranteed to create a lasting impression and a hunger for more.

Olive Oil and Wine Tasting

Olive oil and wine tasting in Sirmione is not just a culinary experience; it's a journey through the rich history, culture, and tradition of the region, offering visitors a chance to sample some of the finest olive oils and wines produced in northern Italy while learning about the art of cultivation, production, and tasting from local experts and artisans.

Olive oil production has been a cornerstone of Sirmione's economy and culture for generations, with the region's warm temperature and rich soil offering perfect circumstances for cultivating olives. Today, Sirmione is home to large olive trees and olive oil mills, where olives are gathered by hand and pressed into fragrant, aromatic oils that are valued for their purity and quality.

During an olive oil tasting session in Sirmione, tourists get the chance to try a selection of extra virgin olive oils, each with its distinct flavor profile, scent, and character. From delicate and sweet oils with traces of green grass and artichoke to strong and peppery oils with a lingering aftertaste, the diversity of tastes and textures is guaranteed to thrill the tongue and stimulate the senses.

In addition to sampling olive oil on its own, visitors may also taste it coupled with local delicacies such as freshly baked bread, luscious tomatoes, and creamy cheeses, enabling them to experience the complete range of flavors and sensations that olive oil has to offer.

Wine tasting is another popular gastronomic activity in Sirmione, with the area having a rich and storied legacy of winemaking that stretches back to ancient times. The moderate temperature, plentiful sunlight, and excellent soil of Lake Garda's shoreline give perfect circumstances for growing grapes, with the area producing a range of wines ranging from crisp whites and fruity rosés to full-bodied reds.

During a wine-tasting trip in Sirmione, tourists may try a range of wines from local vineyards and wineries, including traditional varietals like as Lugana, Bardolino, and Valpolicella. Guided by trained sommeliers and winemakers, guests may learn about the distinctive qualities of each wine, including its scent, taste profile, and age potential, as well as the processes and traditions that go into its creation.

In addition to sampling wines, guests may also enjoy guided tours of local vineyards and wineries, where they can learn about the grape growing process, the art of winemaking, and the history and culture of wine production in the area. From wandering through the vineyards and viewing the cellars to enjoying panoramic views of the countryside and drinking wines directly from the barrel, a wine-tasting trip in Sirmione gives a unique and fascinating peek into the world of Italian winemaking.

Whether you're a seasoned expert or a curious beginner, olive oil and wine tasting in Sirmione is likely to be a wonderful and instructive experience, offering a greater understanding of the tastes, scents, and traditions of this charming corner of Italy. So come, raise a glass, and salute the rich culinary legacy of Sirmione, where every sip and every taste tells a narrative of love, artistry, and tradition.

Best Restaurants and Local Eateries

Sirmione features a rich culinary scene, with a broad choice of restaurants and small eateries serving everything from classic Italian food to contemporary fusion cuisine. Here are some of the top restaurants and eateries in Sirmione, along with their precise address details:

Ristorante La Speranzina:
Address: Via Speranzina, 2, 25019 Sirmione BS, Italy
Situated on the beaches of Lake Garda, Ristorante La Speranzina provides a lovely setting with spectacular views of the lake. The restaurant specializes in seafood dishes produced using locally obtained products, as well as classic Italian cuisine with a modern touch. Guests may eat on the balcony overlooking the water or in the exquisite dining room, tasting meals such as risotto with lake fish, grilled seafood platters, and handmade pasta.

Ristorante Antica Cascina San Zago:
Address: Via San Zeno, 25, 25019 Sirmione BS, Italy
Located in a lovely farmhouse surrounded by vineyards and olive trees, Ristorante Antica Cascina San Zago provides a comfortable and rustic

ambiance. The menu comprises a range of typical Lombard meals, including handmade pasta, grilled meats, and substantial stews, as well as a selection of local wines and cheeses. Guests may eat inside by the fireplace or outside on the patio, enjoying magnificent views of the countryside.

Trattoria Clementina:
Address: Via Colombare, 27, 25019 Sirmione BS, Italy
Tucked away on a quiet lane in the Colombare area, Trattoria Clementina is a favorite among residents and travelers alike. The restaurant delivers traditional Italian food produced with fresh, locally sourced ingredients, including handcrafted pasta, wood-fired pizzas, and seasonal specialties. Guests may eat in the intimate dining room or on the outside terrace, taking in the attractive decor and pleasant mood.

Osteria al Torcol:
Address: Via Verona, 16, 25019 Sirmione BS, Italy
Nestled in the ancient center of Sirmione, Osteria al Torcol is a typical trattoria noted for its friendly welcome and delicious, home-cooked meals. The menu contains a range of traditional Italian meals, including gnocchi with gorgonzola sauce, osso buco with saffron risotto, and tiramisu for dessert.

Guests may eat inside in the quaint dining room or outside on the lovely terrace, enjoying views of the lively streets.

Trattoria La Fiasca:
Address: Via Scala, 11, 25019 Sirmione BS, Italy
Situated only feet from the Scaliger Castle, Trattoria La Fiasca is a family-run restaurant that specializes in authentic Venetian food. The menu contains a range of seafood dishes, including risotto with shrimp and clams, grilled sea bass, and squid ink pasta, as well as handcrafted sweets such as tiramisu and panna cotta. Guests may eat inside in the comfortable dining room or outside on the terrace, enjoying views of the castle and the lake beyond.

These are just a handful of the many great restaurants and cafes that Sirmione has to offer. Whether you're wanting fresh seafood, handmade pasta, or a typical Italian pizza, you're sure to find something wonderful to satiate your hunger in this quaint lakeside town.

Chapter 7. Practical Information for Visitors

Transportation in Sirmione

Transportation in Sirmione elegantly integrates practicality with the elegance of the town's ancient streets and picturesque environs, allowing guests a range of alternatives for getting about and experiencing this wonderful location. From walking and cycling to public transit and boat trips, Sirmione offers accessible and effective means to explore its tiny streets, charming promenades, and breathtaking countryside.

Walking: With its modest size and pedestrian-friendly streets, walking is one of the greatest ways to discover Sirmione. Visitors may meander down the medieval cobblestone streets of the old town, soaking in the sights and sounds of ages past as they browse past lovely shops, cafés, and historic buildings. Walking also enables tourists to uncover hidden jewels and off-the-beaten-path sights that may not be accessible by conventional forms of transportation.

Riding: For those seeking to discover Sirmione and its surrounding countryside at a speedier pace, riding is a popular alternative. The town is equipped with a network of bike trails and riding routes that weave through the lovely countryside, affording breathtaking vistas of vineyards, olive groves, and old homes along the way. Visitors may hire bicycles from local shops or hotels and start on self-guided cycling excursions of the region, pausing to explore quaint towns, sip local wines, and enjoy leisurely picnics among the majesty of nature.

Public Transportation: Sirmione is well linked to other towns and cities in the region by public transportation, making it convenient for travelers to explore the surrounding area. The town is serviced by local buses that link it to surrounding towns such as Desenzano del Garda, Peschiera del Garda, and Verona, as well as regional trains that give access to larger cities like as Milan, Venice, and Florence. Additionally, ferries and water taxis operate on Lake Garda, giving picturesque tours and transit to various lakefront towns and attractions.

Taxi and Ride-Sharing Services: Taxis are widely accessible in Sirmione and may be hailed on the street or booked in advance via local taxi firms. Additionally, ride-sharing services such as Uber and Lyft operate in the region, offering handy transit choices for those who prefer the flexibility and convenience of app-based transportation services.

Boat Tours: Exploring Sirmione and Lake Garda by boat is a popular and enjoyable way to see the beauty of the area. Boat trips and cruises leave daily from Sirmione's dock, allowing guests the chance to sail around the lake's pure waters, see quaint lakeside towns, and observe stunning views of the surrounding mountains and countryside. Whether you select a leisurely sightseeing cruise or an exciting sailing trip, a boat tour is guaranteed to be a highlight of your vacation to Sirmione.

In conclusion, transportation in Sirmione gives guests a range of practical and efficient solutions for moving about and visiting this lovely area. Whether you choose to wander along cobblestone streets, bike through the countryside, or cruise along the lake's beautiful waters, Sirmione delivers the right combination of convenience, charm, and visual beauty for an outstanding vacation experience.

Accommodation Options

Sirmione provides a broad selection of lodging alternatives to suit every taste, budget, and inclination, from elegant waterfront hotels to beautiful bed & breakfasts and modest guesthouses. Whether you're looking for a romantic hideaway, a family-friendly resort, or a budget-friendly alternative, Sirmione offers something for everyone. Here are some of the housing alternatives in Sirmione, along with their precise address details:

Grand Hotel Terme:
Address: Via Brescia, 5, 25019 Sirmione BS, Italy
   Situated on the banks of Lake Garda, Grand Hotel Terme is a beautiful five-star hotel that provides exquisite suites, world-class services, and breathtaking views of the lake. The hotel has large guest rooms and suites with contemporary decor, marble baths, and private balconies overlooking the lake. Guests may enjoy a selection of facilities, including a spa and wellness center, indoor and outdoor pools, and gourmet dining choices.

Hotel Sirmione e Promessi Sposi:
Address: Piazza Castello, 19, 25019 Sirmione BS, Italy

Located in the heart of Sirmione's historic district, Hotel Sirmione e Promessi Sposi is a lovely four-star hotel built in a historic edifice dating back to the 19th century. The hotel provides comfortable and attractive accommodations, with large guest rooms and suites boasting contemporary conveniences and traditional Italian design. Guests may relax at the hotel's rooftop terrace overlooking the town and enjoy free breakfast provided in the exquisite dining room.

Hotel Olivi Thermae & Natural Spa:
Address: Via San Martino della Battaglia, 7, 25019 Sirmione BS, Italy

Nestled between beautiful gardens and olive trees, Hotel Olivi Thermae & Natural Spa is a calm paradise that provides a peaceful respite from the rush and bustle of daily life. The hotel provides beautiful guest rooms and suites with contemporary facilities, as well as a full-service spa and wellness center with thermal pools, saunas, and massage treatments. Guests may also enjoy free breakfast provided on the hotel's lovely patio.

Hotel Eden:
Address: Via Cavour, 2, 25019 Sirmione BS, Italy

Located just steps from the beaches of Lake Garda, Hotel Eden is a family-run hotel that provides friendly hospitality, pleasant rooms, and spectacular views of the lake. The hotel includes charming guest rooms with classic design and contemporary facilities, as well as a rooftop terrace with panoramic views of the sea and surrounding landscape. Guests may enjoy free breakfast provided in the hotel's dining room and relax in the garden courtyard.

Residence Il Sogno:
Address: Via Dei Pioppi, 1, 25019 Sirmione BS, Italy
   Ideal for families and parties, Residence Il Sogno provides large and completely furnished apartments with contemporary conveniences and private balconies overlooking the lake. The property offers a swimming pool, sun deck, and manicured grounds, as well as a children's playground and BBQ amenities. Guests may enjoy the freedom of self-catering rooms while also having access to hotel-like facilities and services.

These are just a handful of the various hotel choices available in Sirmione. Whether you're seeking elegance, comfort, or affordability, you're sure to find the right spot to stay in this picturesque lakeside town.

Shopping and Souvenirs

Shopping in Sirmione is a lovely experience that allows tourists the chance to explore a variety of beautiful shops, boutiques, and markets while finding unique treasures and souvenirs to take home as treasured keepsakes of their stay in this enchanting city. From locally created crafts and artisanal items to designer clothing and gourmet snacks, Sirmione's retail scene offers something for everyone. Here's a thorough overview of shopping and souvenir alternatives in Sirmione:

Old Town Stores & Boutiques: Sirmione's ancient old town is home to a multitude of charming stores and boutiques that line its narrow cobblestone alleys, providing a broad range of items ranging from handmade pottery and ceramics to locally produced olive oil and wine. Visitors may visit lovely artisan workshops and galleries, where they can observe expert artisans at work and buy one-of-a-kind mementos such as hand-painted tiles, leather products, and jewelry. Additionally, there are various stores providing designer apparel, shoes, and accessories, enabling fashion fans to indulge in some retail therapy among the town's gorgeous surroundings.

Local Markets: Throughout the week, Sirmione offers a variety of outdoor markets where tourists may peruse booths bursting with fresh food, local delicacies, and handmade crafts. The weekly market, held every Monday morning in Piazza Mercato, provides a colorful environment and a large choice of products, including fruits, vegetables, cheeses, cured meats, and baked goods, as well as apparel, accessories, and home items. Additionally, there are specialist markets devoted to crafts, antiques, and vintage things, giving unique shopping possibilities for collectors and bargain seekers alike.

Gourmet Food Stores: Food fans will rejoice in the number of gourmet food stores and delicatessens sprinkled around Sirmione, where visitors can try and buy a range of local delicacies and culinary pleasures. From freshly baked bread and pastries to artisanal cheeses, cured meats, and regional wines, these businesses provide a tempting selection of items that represent the tastes and traditions of Lake Garda's culinary history. Visitors may also discover a range of delicious gift baskets and memento packs, ideal for tasting Sirmione home with them.

Souvenir Stores: For those seeking traditional souvenirs and mementos, Sirmione provides a choice of souvenir stores and gift shops that offer a range of regionally themed products and trinkets. Visitors may explore shelves packed with postcards, magnets, keychains, and other tiny tokens emblazoned with photographs of Sirmione's sites and attractions, as well as handmade ceramics, glassware, and fabrics exhibiting designs inspired by the region's rich history and natural beauty. Additionally, specialized stores are selling handcrafted soaps, fragrances, and skincare goods manufactured with locally derived materials, enabling tourists to indulge themselves with a touch of Lake Garda grandeur.

Lakeside Promenade: The lakeside promenade of Sirmione provides a gorgeous location for leisurely shopping and walking, with a variety of outdoor sellers and street entertainers contributing to the vibrant ambiance. Visitors may peruse kiosks offering homemade crafts, jewelry, artwork, and souvenirs, as well as enjoy local street food delicacies like gelato, croissants, and roasted chestnuts. The promenade is also a popular area for artists and crafters to show their work, allowing chances for tourists to acquire unique works of art and support the local creative community.

In conclusion, shopping in Sirmione gives tourists a fascinating combination of culture, craftsmanship, and gastronomic pleasures, delivering a memorable and gratifying experience for anyone wishing to explore the town's dynamic retail scene. Whether you're hunting for unusual souvenirs, delicious snacks, or fashionable apparel, Sirmione offers something to suit every taste and budget, guaranteeing that your shopping expedition is a highlight of your visit to this picturesque lakeside town.

Safety Tips and Emergency Contacts

Ensuring the safety and well-being of guests is a high concern in Sirmione, and the town is well-equipped with resources and services to manage situations and give aid when required. Whether you're touring the town's historic buildings, enjoying outdoor activities, or consuming local food, it's vital to take basic steps to guarantee a safe and happy trip. Here are some safety guidelines and emergency contacts to keep in mind during your stay in Sirmione:

General Safety Tips: -
Stay mindful of your surroundings and avoid roaming alone in new locations, particularly at night.

Keep your valuables safe at all times and be careful against pickpocketing and theft, especially in popular tourist locations.

Stay hydrated and protect yourself from the heat by wearing sunscreen, a hat, and sunglasses, particularly during the summer months when temperatures may be high. - Follow local safety standards and requirements while engaging in outdoor activities such as swimming, boating, and hiking, and always wear proper safety gear and equipment.

Water Safety: - While swimming in Lake Garda may be a relaxing and delightful experience, it's necessary to exercise care and stick to safety requirements, particularly if you're not a good swimmer.

Choose authorized swimming locations with lifeguards on duty, and never swim alone or in regions where swimming is forbidden.

Be wary of underwater dangers such as rocks, currents, and drop-offs, and avoid diving into shallow water or unknown depths.

If engaging in water sports or activities, be sure to wear a life jacket or other flotation device and follow safety advice issued by instructors or guides.

Medical Emergencies: -
In the case of a medical emergency, phone the European emergency number 112 to seek help from emergency services such as paramedics, police, or firefighters. - Sirmione is equipped with many medical facilities, including hospitals, clinics, and pharmacies, where tourists may obtain medical care and treatment if needed.
It's a good idea to have a copy of your medical insurance information and any essential prescriptions with you at all times, as well as a list

of emergency contacts in case of unanticipated medical concerns.

Lost or Taken Property: -
If you lose expensive possessions or have items taken during your vacation, notify the event to the local police station or tourist information center as soon as possible to submit a complaint and seek help.

Keep copies of crucial papers such as passports, identity cards, and trip plans in a secure location away from your primary things, and consider utilizing a money belt or concealed pouch to hold valuables while visiting the area.

Emergency Contacts:
Emergency Services: 112 (European emergency number)
Police: 113
Medical Emergencies: 118
Fire Department: 115
Tourist Information Center: +39 030 916 110

In conclusion, by following these safety precautions and familiarizing yourself with emergency contacts, you can assist in ensuring a safe and happy vacation to Sirmione. Remember to be educated, keep cautious, and prioritize your well-being at all times, enabling you to make the most of your visit to this lovely lakeside town.

Chapter 8. Itineraries and Day Trips

One-Day Itinerary: Highlights of Sirmione

Crafting a one-day plan to visit the attractions of Sirmione is like beginning a trip through time, culture, and natural beauty. This gorgeous town set on the shores of Lake Garda provides a plethora of attractions, from old ruins and historic sites to breathtaking promenades and attractive cafés. Here's a thorough plan to make the most of your day in Sirmione:

Morning:
Start your day with a visit to Scaliger Castle, a medieval fortification that stands as a sentry at the gateway to Sirmione's ancient town. Explore the castle's magnificent walls, towers, and courtyards, then climb to the top for panoramic views of the town and lake below.

After viewing the castle, meander around the small alleyways of Sirmione's old town, taking in the ambiance and appreciating the wonderful architecture. Stop by the Chiesa di San Pietro in Mavino, one of the town's oldest churches, and enjoy its historic paintings and Romanesque architecture.

Head towards the northern extremity of the peninsula to view the Grotte di Catullo, the remnants of a large Roman villa overlooking the lake. Explore the archeological site and envision life in ancient times as you meander amid the decaying walls and columns.

Lunch:
For lunch, travel to one of Sirmione's waterfront restaurants or cafés to enjoy a leisurely meal with wonderful views of the lake. Sample local favorites such as risotto al pesce, trota alla gardesana, or handmade pasta with fresh shellfish, followed by a glass of local wine.

Afternoon:
After lunch, take a leisurely walk along the lakeside promenade, enjoying the gorgeous vistas and soft air. Stop to view the lovely Scaligeri Harbor and observe the colorful boats bobbing in the sea.

Continue your trek to the Terme di Sirmione, a historic thermal spa noted for its therapeutic waters and health therapies. Take a guided tour of the spa's amenities, including thermal pools, saunas, and relaxation spaces, and learn about the therapeutic effects of the mineral-rich waters.

If time permits, hire a pedal boat or kayak and explore the serene waters of Lake Garda at your leisure, taking in the beauty of the surrounding landscape and enjoying the tranquility of the lake.

Evening:
As the sun starts to drop, make your way back to the old town to experience the wonderful golden hour spreading a warm light over the cobblestone streets and antique buildings. Stop by a gelateria for a scoop of luscious gelato or have a sunset aperitivo at a waterfront pub, relishing the moment and reminiscing on the day's activities.

Finally, indulge in a delightful evening at one of Sirmione's finest restaurants, experiencing the tastes of classic Italian food cooked with locally sourced ingredients. Toast to a fantastic day in Sirmione and cherish every minute before waving goodbye to this lovely town.

By following this one-day itinerary, you'll have the chance to explore the finest of Sirmione's history, culture, and natural beauty, leaving you with lasting memories and a wish to return to this delightful lakeside paradise.

Two-Day Adventure: Exploring Lake Garda

Embarking on a two-day excursion to visit Lake Garda provides a wonderful combination of leisure, exploration, and outdoor activities. With its gorgeous scenery, attractive villages, and rich cultural legacy, Lake Garda is a treasure trove waiting to be found. Here's a comprehensive schedule for a fantastic two-day excursion experiencing the wonders of Lake Garda:

Day 1: Southern Shores of Lake Garda

Morning:
Start your day with a picturesque drive or boat trip to the southern beaches of Lake Garda, where you'll discover the lovely village of Sirmione. Explore the medieval old town, explore Scaliger Castle and meander among the ancient remains of the Grotte di Catullo.

After touring Sirmione, drive to neighboring Desenzano del Garda, the biggest town on the lake. Stroll along the lakeside promenade, see the historic town, and climb the Rocca di Desenzano for panoramic views of the lake and surrounding landscape.

Lunch:
Enjoy a leisurely lunch at one of Desenzano's waterfront eateries, savoring local delicacies like as risotto al pesce, grilled lake fish, or handmade pasta with pesto. Pair your dinner with a glass of Lugana wine, a crisp white wine made in the area.

Afternoon:
In the afternoon, tour the charming town of Garda, situated on the eastern coast of the lake. Take a stroll along the lakeside promenade, see the lovely Piazza Catullo, and peruse the stores and boutiques in the old center.

If time permits, take a boat trip to the lake to see the lovely village of Bardolino, noted for its vineyards and olive trees. Sample local wines at a vineyard, see the Church of San Severo and wander around the town's lovely parks and gardens.

Evening:
Return to Desenzano del Garda for supper and have a meal at one of the town's vibrant trattorias or pizzerias. Savor typical Italian cuisines such as

pasta carbonara, tagliatelle al ragù, or pizza margherita, accompanied by a glass of local wine.

After supper, take a leisurely walk down the lakefront promenade and watch the sunset over the water, appreciating the beauty and peace of Lake Garda.

Day 2: Northern Shores of Lake Garda

Morning:
Start your second day with a visit to the lovely village of Malcesine, situated on the northeastern bank of Lake Garda. Ride the cable car to the summit of Monte Baldo for stunning views of the lake and surrounding mountains.

Explore the old center of Malcesine, see the Scaliger Castle, and meander through the tiny lanes dotted with shops, cafés, and gelaterias.

Lunch:
Enjoy a picturesque lunch at one of Malcesine's waterfront restaurants, taking in the spectacular views of the lake and mountains. Sample local delicacies such as lake fish roasted over an open flame, handmade pasta with truffles, or polenta with mushrooms and cheese.

Afternoon:
After lunch, enjoy a boat trip to the lake to explore the picturesque village of Limone sul Garda, noted for its lemon orchards and colorful coastline. Explore the town's small alleyways, see the Church of San Benedetto, and drink Limoncello, a lemon liqueur created with locally cultivated lemons.

If time permits, take a plunge in the soothing waters of Lake Garda or sit on one of the town's sandy beaches, soaking up the sun and admiring the tranquil beauty of the lake.

Evening:
Return to Malcesine for supper and have a meal at one of the town's charming trattorias or gourmet eateries. Indulge in delicious seafood meals, handcrafted pasta, and sumptuous desserts, complemented with a bottle of regional wine.

After dinner, take a leisurely walk along the lakeside promenade and experience the busy nightlife of Malcesine, with live music, street performers, and crowded cafés and bars.

By following this two-day itinerary, you'll have the chance to see the attractions of Lake Garda, from quaint villages and ancient buildings to stunning landscapes and outdoor activities, leaving you with treasured memories of your journey on Italy's biggest lake.

Beyond Sirmione: Day Trips to Nearby Attractions

Venturing outside Sirmione brings up a world of opportunities for thrilling day excursions to local locations, each presenting its distinct combination of history, culture, and natural beauty. From attractive cities and ancient buildings to gorgeous landscapes and outdoor experiences, the surrounding region of Lake Garda is ready for exploration. Here's a comprehensive plan for day visits to local destinations beyond Sirmione:

Day Trip 1: Verona and Valpolicella Wine Region

Morning:
Begin your day with a gorgeous drive or train trip to the old city of Verona, situated only a short distance from Sirmione. Explore the city's UNESCO-listed medieval center, explore prominent sights such as the Arena di Verona, Juliet's House, and Piazza delle Erbe, and walk along the lovely Adige River.

Lunch:
Enjoy a leisurely lunch at one of Verona's lovely trattorias or osterias, tasting classic Italian specialties such as risotto al nero di seppia, bistecca

alla fiorentina, or tortellini in brodo. Pair your dinner with a glass of Valpolicella wine, a rich red wine made in the adjacent Valpolicella wine area.

Afternoon:
After lunch, continue on a guided tour of the Valpolicella wine area, noted for its scenic vines, ancient wineries, and world-class wines. Visit famous vineyards such as Allegrini, Bertani, or Serego Alighieri, where you can explore the cellars, learn about the winemaking process, and taste a selection of Valpolicella wines.

Evening:
Return to Sirmione in the evening and relax at one of the town's waterfront restaurants or cafés, eating a superb supper and watching the sunset over Lake Garda. Reflect on the day's events and cherish the memories of your visit to Verona and the Valpolicella wine region.

Day Trip 2: Dolomite Mountains and Trentino-Alto Adige Region

Morning:
Wake up early and go on a picturesque drive or guided excursion to the spectacular Dolomite Mountains, situated to the north of Lake Garda.

Marvel at the majestic peaks, craggy cliffs, and alpine meadows as you make your way through this stunning UNESCO World Heritage Site.

Lunch:
Stop for lunch at a classic mountain rifugio or alpine restaurant, where you may eat robust mountain food such as polenta with wild mushrooms, speck and cheese platters, or handmade apple strudel. Enjoy magnificent views of the surrounding mountains as you eat among the gorgeous natural landscape.

Afternoon:
Continue your tour of the Dolomites with a guided trek or scenic drive across the region's stunning valleys and mountain passes. Visit picturesque towns like Canazei, Cortina d'Ampezzo, or Ortisei, where you can explore local stores, appreciate old architecture, and absorb the laid-back alpine ambiance.

Evening:
Return to Sirmione in the evening and unwind with a pleasant supper at one of the town's charming restaurants or trattorias. Indulge in substantial Italian comfort cuisine such as gnocchi with

gorgonzola sauce, ossobuco alla milanese, or tiramisu, followed by a glass of local wine.

By following these day trip itineraries, you'll have the chance to experience the different sights and natural beauty of the surrounding region beyond Sirmione, leaving you with treasured memories of your travels in northern Italy.

Chapter 9. Tips for a Memorable Stay

Photography Tips for Capturing Sirmione's Beauty

Capturing the beauty of Sirmione via photography is a pleasurable task, as this gorgeous town provides a plethora of breathtaking vistas, ancient sites, and charming details ready to be preserved in photos. Whether you're a beginner photographer or a seasoned expert, here are some photography suggestions to help you make the most of your time in Sirmione and take great images that will serve as lasting souvenirs of your stay:

Golden Hour Magic: Take advantage of the magnificent light during the golden hour, which happens during the first hour after dawn and the final hour before sunset. During this time, the gentle, warm light provides a wonderful glow that highlights the colors and textures of Sirmione's landscapes and buildings. Plan your photographic expeditions appropriately to capture the town drenched in golden light, whether it's the gentle colors of daybreak over Lake Garda or the warm tones of sunset shining off Scaliger Castle.

Explore New Viewpoints: Don't be hesitant to experiment with new angles, compositions, and viewpoints to get unique and interesting images of Sirmione. Get down low to the ground for intriguing foreground objects, photograph from high vantage points for sweeping views of the town and lake, and search for reflections in the water or glass surfaces to add visual interest to your photos. By exploring various views, you'll find new ways to exhibit Sirmione's beauty and make intriguing images.

Focus on Nuances: While Sirmione's prominent sights such as Scaliger Castle and the Grotte di Catullo surely deserve your attention, don't neglect the minor nuances that add to the town's charm and character. Pay attention to architectural features, colorful doors and windows, beautiful brickwork, and blossoming flowers that bring individuality to the streets and buildings. These elements may make for fascinating close-up images and add depth and character to your photography.

Embrace the Seasons: Sirmione's beauty varies with the seasons, allowing various picture possibilities throughout the year. In spring, capture the town decked with flowering flowers and vivid greenery, while in summer, snap the lively ambiance of lakeside cafés and busy streets. Fall gives spectacular foliage colors, while winter offers a calmer, more intimate environment with the town decked in seasonal decorations. Embrace the seasonal changes and capture Sirmione's beauty in all its seasonal splendor.

Capture the Spirit of Daily Life: Beyond the renowned monuments and postcard-perfect panoramas, seek to capture the spirit of daily life in Sirmione via your photographs. Candid street scenes, local merchants in the market, fishermen on the lake, and locals going about their daily routines all give possibilities to chronicle the real charm and character of the town. These genuine moments add dimension and narrative to your photographs, enabling viewers to connect with the soul of Sirmione.

Experiment with Light and Shadow: Use light and shadow to your advantage to produce dramatic and emotive images of Sirmione. Play with backlighting to silhouette figures against the sky or water, play with dappled light streaming through vegetation, and embrace the contrast between light and shadow to give depth and texture to your photographs. By understanding the interplay of light and shadow, you may improve your photography and produce photos that generate emotion and capture the spectator.

Don't Forget the Night Sky: Sirmione's splendor continues into the night, allowing magnificent evening photography. Capture the town lighted by the warm glow of streetlights, the shimmering lights of lakefront cafés and restaurants, and the starry sky above. Experiment with long exposure methods to capture the action of the water or the tracks of passing boats, and consider integrating features like reflections and silhouettes to add interest to your evening shots.

Convey a Tale: Lastly, attempt to convey a captivating tale via your photos by building a unified narrative that captures the spirit of your time in Sirmione. Think beyond individual shots and analyze how your photographs work together to communicate the tone, ambiance, and beauty of the place. Whether you're filming a day in the life of Sirmione or capturing the timeless attraction of its historic monuments, try to create a visual tale that connects with viewers and takes them to this lovely lakeside resort.

By following these photography techniques and embracing the beauty and character of Sirmione, you'll be able to take breathtaking photographs that serve as treasured mementos of your stay in this enchanting town. Whether you're exploring the old alleyways, appreciating the magnificent views of Lake Garda, or just soaking in the ambiance, let your imagination and love for photography lead you as you preserve the beauty of Sirmione for generations to come.

Packing Essentials for Different Seasons

Packing for a great visit in Sirmione takes careful consideration of the seasonal weather, local activities, and personal tastes. Whether you're traveling in the hot days of summer or the snug ambiance of winter, having the appropriate items will improve your experience and guarantee a comfortable and pleasurable stay. Here are some packing necessities customized to various seasons in Sirmione:

Spring (March to May):
Lightweight Clothes: Spring in Sirmione provides warm temperatures and occasional rains, so pack a range of lightweight clothes including long-sleeved shirts, sweaters, and a waterproof jacket or windbreaker.
Comfortable Walking Shoes: Explore Sirmione's cobblestone streets and gorgeous promenades with ease by carrying comfortable walking shoes or sneakers with excellent grip.
Sun Protection: While spring temperatures are moderate, the sun may still be powerful, so don't forget to take sunscreen, sunglasses, and a wide-brimmed hat to protect yourself from UV rays.

Umbrella or Raincoat: Be prepared for periodic rains by carrying an umbrella or lightweight raincoat to remain dry while touring the town and surrounding region.

Summer (June to August):
Lightweight Clothes: Summer in Sirmione is characterized by high temperatures and sunny days, so bring lightweight, breathable clothes such as shorts, t-shirts, sundresses, and swimwear.
Sunscreen and Sun Protection: Protect yourself from the sun's rays by carrying sunscreen with a high SPF, sunglasses, a wide-brimmed hat, and a lightweight cover-up or sarong for added protection.
Beach Needs: If you want to spend time at the beach, don't forget to bring a beach towel, swimsuit, flip-flops, or sandals, and a beach bag to carry your needs.
Water Bottle: Stay hydrated in the summer heat by bringing a refillable water bottle and filling it up at the various water fountains and public taps strewn around Sirmione.
Camera and Accessories: Capture memories of your summer experiences in Sirmione by carrying a camera or smartphone with lots of storage capacity, along with additional batteries and memory cards.

Fall (September to November):

Layered apparel: Fall brings lower weather and changing foliage to Sirmione, so pack a combination of lightweight layers and warmer apparel such as sweaters, jeans, long-sleeved shirts, and a light jacket or coat.

Comfortable Shoes: Explore Sirmione's gorgeous streets and rural paths with comfortable walking shoes or boots that give support and grip on rough terrain.

Umbrella or Raincoat: Fall rains are prevalent in Sirmione, so be prepared for rain by carrying an umbrella or waterproof jacket to remain dry while touring the town and surrounding region.

Fall Accessories: Stay comfy and elegant in Sirmione's fall weather by carrying accessories such as scarves, gloves, and a knit cap to stay warm on chilly days and nights.

Winter (December to February):

Warm Layers: Winter in Sirmione offers low temperatures and sometimes frost, so pack warm layers like sweaters, thermal underwear, wool socks, and a thick coat or parka to be comfy in the cold.

Winter Accessories: Don't forget to carry winter accessories such as a scarf, gloves, and a knit hat to remain warm and protect yourself from the weather while touring Sirmione's medieval streets and lakeside promenades.

Waterproof Boots: Navigate Sirmione's cobblestone walkways and possibly ice paths with ease by carrying waterproof boots with sufficient grip to keep your feet warm and dry in the winter weather.

Indoor Activities: Plan for indoor activities on cold days by carrying books, puzzles, or electronic gadgets to keep yourself busy during downtime at your hotel or when cozying up in a lakeside café.

Regardless of the season, it's always a good idea to bring important goods such as travel papers, medicine, toiletries, and a travel adaptor if required. By preparing intelligently and considering the seasonal weather and local activities, you can ensure a memorable and pleasurable stay in Sirmione, no matter the time of year.

Chapter 10. Conclusion

Farewell to Sirmione

As your stay in Sirmione comes to a close, it's normal to feel a feeling of bittersweet nostalgia for the memories built and experiences shared in this charming lakeside town. Saying goodbye to Sirmione is not only about saying adieu to a place; it's about reflecting on the moments of wonder, discovery, and connection that have enriched your trip and left an everlasting stamp on your heart and spirit. Here's a sincere goodbye to Sirmione, reflecting the spirit of your great experience:

As the sun sets over the serene waters of Lake Garda, throwing a golden light onto the historic walls of Scaliger Castle and the quaint alleys of Sirmione, it's time to send a fond goodbye to this enchanting corner of Italy. With each stride down the cobblestone streets, among the aroma of blossoming flowers and the sound of laughter resounding through the air, memories of your time in Sirmione fill your memory like the soft waves lapping at the coast.

Farewell, Sirmione, with your timeless beauty and ancient charm that have grabbed the hearts of pilgrims for generations. From the majestic castle of Scaliger Castle to the ancient ruins of the Grotte di Catullo, you've unveiled the layers of your rich history and cultural legacy, encouraging us to stroll through the halls of time and picture the lives of those who came before.

Farewell, Sirmione, with its quiet lakeside promenades and beautiful panoramas that have inspired painters, poets, and dreamers alike. From the dazzling waters of Lake Garda to the green hillsides covered with olive groves and vineyards, you've offered a refuge of natural beauty and calm, enabling us to reconnect with the cycles of the earth and the beauty of the world around us.

Farewell, Sirmione, with your warm hospitality and generous attitude that has greeted us with open arms and made us feel at home in your embrace. From the courteous welcomes of local inhabitants to the delectable scents wafting from busy cafes and trattorias, you've nurtured our bodies and hearts, leaving us with memories of shared laughter, shared meals, and shared moments of delight.

As we say goodbye to Sirmione, we take with us the beloved memories of our time spent in your midst, the friendships established, and the experiences embarked upon. Though our journey may take us far from your beaches, the beauty and wonder of Sirmione will forever stay inscribed in our hearts, a beacon of light and inspiration leading us on our route.

Until we meet again, lovely Sirmione, may your old walls stay strong, your waterways remain serene, and your spirit continue to inspire everyone lucky enough to roam within your midst. Grazie Mille for the memories, the laughter, and the love. Arrivederci, Sirmione, till we meet again.

As you say goodbye to Sirmione, may your heart be filled with appreciation for the experiences shared and the memories formed, knowing that the beauty and charm of this lovely town will always stay with you, wherever your travels may take. Grazie e arrivederci, sweet Sirmione.

Appendix

Glossary of Italian Terms

As you complete your tour through Sirmione and its surrounding areas, it's useful to reflect on the rich tapestry of Italian culture and language that has imbued your experience with depth and authenticity. From the lyrical melodies of Italian talks to the delectable aromas of local food, Italy's language and customs offer a dynamic depth to every minute spent in this wonderful place. To help in your knowledge and admiration of Italian culture, here is a complete lexicon of Italian terminology, spanning from common idioms to gastronomic pleasures and cultural concepts:

Buongiorno: Good morning.
Buonasera: Good evening.
Grazie: Thank you.
Prego: You're welcome.
Ciao: Hello/goodbye (casual).
Arrivederci: Goodbye.
Piazza: Town square or plaza.
Gelato: Italian ice cream, famed for its creamy texture and rich taste.

Trattoria: Casual Italian eatery delivering classic handcrafted cuisine.

Ristorante: Formal Italian restaurant with a comprehensive menu of regional delicacies.

Antipasto: Appetizer or appetizer meal often consisting of cured meats, cheeses, and seasoned vegetables.

Primo: First course, generally pasta, risotto, or soup.

Secondo: Second course, often meat or fish, served with a side dish of vegetables or salad.

Dolce: Dessert.

Caffè: Coffee, generally savored as a rapid shot of espresso or as a leisurely cappuccino or latte.

Aperitivo: Pre-dinner drink or cocktail offered with small nibbles, aimed to increase the appetite.

Osteria: Traditional Italian tavern or bar offering wine and modest, rustic cuisine.

Agriturismo: Farmhouse lodging offers tourists the chance to experience rural life and local food.

Passeggiata: Leisurely promenade, commonly done in the early evening to chat and enjoy the surroundings.

Vino: Wine, Italy is famous for its numerous and acclaimed wine regions.

Formaggio: Cheese, ranging from creamy mozzarella to aged Parmigiano-Reggiano.

Salumi: Assorted cured meats, such as prosciutto, salami, and bresaola.

Gondola: Traditional Venetian rowing boat, closely linked with the city of Venice.

Opera: Grand musical and dramatic performance, with Italy being the cradle of opera.

Piazza Navona: One of Rome's most renowned squares, famed for its spectacular Baroque architecture and bustling ambiance.

Carnevale: Carnival celebration, with Venice staging one of the world's most renowned Carnevale events.

Palazzo: Palace or stately edifice, particularly associated with Italian royalty and nobility.

Vittorio Emanuele II: King of Italy from 1861 to 1878, notable for his role in the unification of Italy.

La Dolce Vita: "The sweet life," an Italian expression referring to a lifestyle of leisure, pleasure, and indulgence.

Ciao Bella: "Hello, beautiful," a cordial greeting typically used to convey appreciation or devotion.

As you study this dictionary of Italian terminology, may it serve as a reminder of the rich cultural fabric that has enriched your trip through Sirmione and beyond. Whether relishing the delicacies of Italian food, marveling at the grandeur of ancient buildings, or just embracing the warmth and friendliness of the Italian people, may your memories of Italy's language and customs continue to inspire and thrill you for years to come. Grazie e arrivederci, till we meet again in the heart of Italy's wonderful embrace.

Map

As you end your investigation of Sirmione and its neighboring territories, a map serves as a great tool to summarize the geographical context of your adventure and the many attractions you've experienced along the route. From the historic features of Sirmione's old town to the picturesque grandeur of Lake Garda and the adjacent towns and villages, a map gives a visual depiction of the landscapes, streets, and sites of interest that have impacted your trip. Here, we give a thorough map of Sirmione and its surrounds, presenting an overview of the area's key attractions and significant landmarks:

Scaliger Castle: Dominating the entrance to Sirmione's ancient town, Scaliger Castle is a medieval fortification with a dominating appearance. Explore its old walls, towers, and courtyards, and enjoy panoramic views of the town and lake from the summit.

Grotte di Catullo: Located near the northern extremity of the Sirmione peninsula, the Grotte di Catullo are the remains of a splendid Roman villa dating back to the 1st century BCE. Explore the archeological site and experience the breathtaking views of Lake Garda from this ancient vantage point.

Chiesa di San Pietro in Mavino: Nestled between olive orchards on the outskirts of Sirmione, the Chiesa di San Pietro in Mavino is one of the town's oldest churches, dating back to the 8th century. Admire its old frescoes and Romanesque architecture, and enjoy the tranquil environment of its surroundings.

Lake Garda: Italy's biggest lake, Lake Garda is a spectacular natural playground with a plethora of outdoor sports and visual splendor. From swimming and boating to hiking and cycling, there's something for everyone to enjoy among the lake's crystal-clear waters and scenic coastlines.

Desenzano del Garda: The biggest town on the southern beaches of Lake Garda, Desenzano del Garda is a busy hive of activity with a lively waterfront promenade, historic center, and thriving eating and nightlife scene. Explore its picturesque alleyways, explore the old Roman villa in the Grotte di Catullo, and absorb the vibrant ambiance of its busy piazzas.

Malcesine: Nestled at the foot of the Dolomite Mountains on the northeastern coast of Lake Garda, Malcesine is a charming town noted for its medieval castle, small lanes, and breathtaking views of the lake and surrounding mountains. Ride the cable car to the summit of Monte Baldo for panoramic views, explore the medieval center, and enjoy the laid-back vibe of this picturesque lakeside town.

Verona: Just a short distance from Sirmione, the historic city of Verona provides a plethora of cultural attractions, including old Roman ruins, Renaissance palaces, and a bustling culinary scene. Visit the magnificent Arena di Verona, wander along the scenic Adige River, and discover the quaint alleys and piazzas of this UNESCO World Heritage-listed city.

Dolomite Mountains: To the north of Sirmione lies the spectacular Dolomite Mountains, a UNESCO World Heritage Site famed for its towering peaks, craggy cliffs, and stunning alpine vistas. Explore charming towns, stroll through verdant valleys, and immerse yourself in the natural splendor of this awe-inspiring mountain range.

As you examine this map of Sirmione and its surroundings, may it serve as a visual memory of the varied attractions and natural beauty that have enhanced your trip through this wonderful area of Italy. Whether visiting ancient ruins, taking in the stunning grandeur of Lake Garda, or immersing yourself in the rich cultural legacy of adjacent towns and villages, may the memories of your travels continue to inspire and excite you for years to come. Grazie e arrivederci, till we meet again within the splendor of Italy's everlasting embrace.

Printed in Great Britain
by Amazon